Lesson's Learned
Pt. 2

<u>*Dedication's*</u>

This book is dedicated to my wife, my kids, my sister's and my friends, new and old. Also to you, the reader's. I appreciate all of you. Continue to read my books and I will continue to write books that appeal to you. Enjoy!
Thank you ALL...

Introduction:

It's been six months since D got shot and I have been there for her 100%. I did everything for her. I was there for her even before the whole Katrina thing. Sure I kept my secrets and maybe even lied to her but hell she was dogging me out the whole time. She cheated on me, and made me feel like shit. Lower than shit. I told her I loved her. She said she loved me too but I guess that was all a lie. These past few months she's been showing me everyday that she's changed her way's, but sometimes I think it's only because she was shot and she finally realized I was the one who was there for her. I guess I can live with that but now I have to find a way to break my news to her and I have to find the right time and place because it could get real ugly. I guess I should tell you how it happened. Here it goes...

Chapter 1:

I met D and was so shocked at how beautiful she was. She was also smart and funny. So I was all in from the start. I had only lived in Cali for six months and she was the first person to fall for me. I had just broke up with my girlfriend that I was with for the past four years. I wasn't quite over her so being with D took my mind away from all the crazy things that had been happening in my life. I had enrolled in school out here and got a job at a preschool. I told D that but what I didn't tell her in all the time that we'd been together was that I also had a night job. This job was how I paid for school and also how I was able to pay my rent and her's when she was on leave from work. I was a stripper and my stage name was Rocky. I almost got caught once but I played it off. One night D was at the club with her friends and they were holding out money for me to come dance with them but I avoided them. The next time I saw them I danced with D and I wanted to tell her but I just couldn't cause I knew it would be all bad. So I continued to avoid them.

D just got a new job which was cool because it gave me a chance to be alone. But my mind is messing with me at this point. I put my all into this relationship. I gave up my past and everything. And she cheated on me numerous times. I feel like that's what I gotta do for me. I know two wrongs don't make a right or does it? I guess I'll find out one day.

It's six o'clock in the evening and I'm bored as hell I'm sitting here looking at T.V. And ain't shit on. I heard key's opening the door and thought it was D but she didn't get off 'till nine o'clock tonight so maybe she got off early. Good thing cause I am horny as hell. I jumped up and slid on my piece and quickly sat back down. I figured if my eyes were closed while I rubbed myself when she walked in she would jump on my lap and to my surprise she did. She started kissing on me but when I opened my eye's it wasn't D, it was Janai. I jumped up and said "what the hell are you doing?" Janai said "well damn, don't act like you didn't know it was me." "Come on man you gotta leave." I said as I tried to fix my boxers. It wasn't working though because the strap that I had just put on on anticipating D's arrival wouldn't let me pull my boxers up. "Why I gotta go? This my best friends house. And you know you wanna fuck or else you wouldn't be sittin here with ya thang on rubbing yourself and shit." She was right I did wanna hit something and anything would work right about now so as she kissed me I could no longer resist myself as I turned her around and bent her over the couch. As I shoved my piece in her I heard her moan. I grabbed her hair and pulled it as I continued to beat her insides harder than I ever had with D. as I smacked her ass and watched it bounce back I thought damn this shit is good. Probably because with D. I make love and take my time. Janai wasn't my girl and I could fuck her as hard as I wanted to. She wasn't my bitch, she was just a quick fuck. I pulled out of her and sat down on the couch and she came and sat down on my lap taking the whole thing in. She began bouncing hard and fast until I could feel all of her juices flowing down her thighs and then she sat on it and laid her head on my shoulder. But shit we wasn't in love and I hadn't got mine yet so I slightly lifted her up and began pounding her from the bottom with her screaming with every push. It passed through my mind that I was killing that shit and I finished right then and there. Hell I was done. It was crazy but I didn't feel that bad about it. I thought I would have but I guess that's what I needed to get passed what D had done to me. I was tired now so I pulled off my piece and told Janai, "A, you gotta bounce now" and to my surprise she didn't trip. She just said "alright well tell D I stopped by and I'll call her later." I guess the look on my face let her know I didn't want D to know cause she said "damn don't trip I ain't gonna say nothing to her, hell I wanted what I just got from you since day one and you gave it to me. Now that I know yo shit is the business like she said. I'm done. We good, don't trip." And with that she walked out the door. Damn she mad cool. Let me fix this couch back up and spray the house before my baby get's home.

Chapter 2:

I was laying on the couch when I decided that I should get up and take a shower. As I got up the phone rang. "What's up"? The number was blocked so I didn't know who it was. Once again I said "Hello"? The person on the other end of the phone said " Hey, how you doing"? I don't believe this shit "Katrina!" I yelled into the phone. "Of course did you think it was your precious D? You know, you a scanless mutha fucker. Her best friend, are you serious?" Click. She hung up the phone. Now this could be a problem. Did she just say she saw me and Janai? Where was she at? Damn. But it will never work. Even if she told, D won't believe her, she know Janai better than that and she know Katrina is crazy and will say anything. But still I gotta play it cool for now. I hopped in the shower and was listening to music when the shower curtain opened. This time it was D standing there naked looking sexy as ever getting ready to hop in with me. Oh Boi! As she got in her breast brushed against my back and I was ready for round 2. she wrapped her arms around me from behind and laid her head on my back. It seemed as if she just wanted to hold me which was cool with me. I asked her "how was work" she sighed when she said " it was OK. I didn't do much." "Well that's cool, so you not tired? Does that mean that Daddy can work you out"? I figured if your gonna cheat it doesn't make since to not still have sex with ya girl. Cause if you don't then she's gonna wonder why you ain't fuckin her and then she's gonna figure your getting it from somewhere else. I turned around and looked in her eye's. She said "naw, never too tired for you daddy" she gave me that sexy ass smile of hers as I picked her up and carried her to the bed. I laid her on the bed and stood in front of her while I reached under the bed for my piece. I slid it on while I nibbled on her stomach. Placing her legs on my shoulders I slid inside of her. I could tell that as I pumped all 10 inches were inside of her because with every stroke our bodies touched and she screamed. As I continued to stroke her in and out she continued to scream how much she loved her daddy. I knew she was talking about me. Hell, I was just that good at what I did. I was in her so long that by the time I finished she couldn't move. We both laid down just the way we were and fell asleep. At about 11:30 I got up and jumped back in the shower. I told D that I was going to kick it with my friends and would be back later. I lied. I was going to the club. I had to work that night. What I didn't know was that D decided to spend time with her friends and hit up the club. So here I am in the dressing room getting ready to hit the floor when I notice there was a card on the table that said "Rocky" I opened it and inside the card it said "watch ya back out there tonight you wouldn't want her to find out." What the hell was this. I put the card in the trash and heard the DJ call me (rocky) to the floor. Sure enough as I walked out there I saw D dancing with Janai and GiGi. Bump it. I gotta do my thing right. Maybe she'll figure it out tonight and I won't have to hide it anymore. So as I moved about the floor I made my way over to D, Janai and GiGi. I grabbed D's hand and picked her up in the air. I continued to dance with her for a while flipping and tossing her here and there. As I got ready to finish the person that was picking up all my tips handed me the basket full of money. I walked off the floor still holding her hand.

When we got in the back I handed her the basket. She said "whats this for? Why did you bring me back here? As she pushed the basket back into my hands. I tried to give it back to her when I said "take it home with you." "Are you crazy? I'm outta here." she said as she walked away. I snatched my mask off and yelled her name "D". She slowly turned around and looked at me. As she walked closer to me I could see the tears forming in her eyes. "So you a stripper? So you been lying to me this whole time, tellin me you out kickin it with your homies huh? You are a fuckin liar. And to think I felt bad about what I did. Here I am trying to make it right with you and be about you and our relationship and you a stripper? I shouldn't even be made at yo ass cause I figured it all ready but no, I pushed those feelings to the side. I told myself that I was the one doin wrong and you was honest and good and you was the best thing that ever happened to me and I was fuckin that up. Well I guess you proved me wrong huh. You ain't so good, right? You got secrets huh? What else you got to tell me Jay? You know what I don't even wanna hear it. I'm outta here." She walked away leaving me standing there looking stupid. But wait a minute, did she forget? Did she really not remember the past year. Is she really callin me the liar in this relationship? She got it twisted. All that shit she put me through. But damn I was foul as hell also. I messed things up from the beginning. I messed up big time she just don't know how much. Hell I was just as foul as her. I don't know what to do. I mean I'm really feeling her and I do love her, it's just I cant get all her wrong doing's out my mind. And it's like I pushed all my mistakes to the side to look at hers. I got dressed and went home. It was one o'clock in the morning and she wasn't home. I was there alone once again looking stupid. About two hours later she came walking through the door with Janai and GiGi laughing and shit. I was nervous thinking Janai was gonna say something to D about what happened but she didn't say anything yet so that was cool. I got up to walk in the room since no one spoke to me when they walked in. But by the time I got close to the hallway D said "slow down *Rocky*, where you going?" She was messing with my head now. "In the room. I'm bout to lay down." She said "damn daddy why you going to bed so early." Early, she was drunk as hell it was early in the morning, three in the morning to be exact. She was slurring when she talked and said " you too tired to take some shots with us." I told her to step in the room with me for a minute. When we got in the room she shoved her tongue in my mouth and when she came up for air she said "look I ain't trippin off that. It hurts yeah. But I'm cool. It just bothered me that you kept it from me. But all that hurt I put you through this past year and you still stayed with me. I can handle this one little lie baby. Now come on in the living room and lets get a little drink on and you can show us some of them dance moves. She grabbed my hand and we walked back into the living room. After a few shots I was in there stripping for all of them. It felt good not to have to hide it anymore. Now I could take my girl with me when I go. While I was dancin Janai came up behind me and tried to dance with me. By this time I was drunk as hell, but drunk or not I could still think straight and I knew this could not be good. This could be real bad. I danced with her but I wasn't gonna be all on her cause I didn't want D to think there was something going on. And I didn't want to not dance with her cause I didn't want D to think I was avoiding Janai for some reason and just to be safe I pulled GiGi and danced with him too. We were all having a good time 'till my phone rang. Unfortunately I wasn't by it, D was. She picked it up and said "hello" I kept on dancing, I had nothing to hide hell I was dancing with one of my secrets and the other one was long gone so I was cool until I looked over at her face. What ever the person was saying on the other end of the phone really pissed her off, cause she started cussing saying "who you calling a bitch? You don't know me. Oh you do? Well if you know me like you say you do then you know where I live. And if you know where I live then you know how to get at me. Bitch" Click. She hung up the phone and looked at me and said "ROOM NOW." GiGi said "oh, oh *Daddy* looks like some body in trouble" D looked at him and said "y'all need to raise up we gotta talk" I guess they got the hint cause they both grabbed their purses and left. I just stood there. After the door closed D said "whats this shit. Some bitch calling your phone talking bout you a dog and I'm a stupid bitch that better watch my back, and you fucking every body and she got proof and shit?" My mind went blank. I can't believe it's happening like this and I gotta think quick. Cause she is pissed. This is just too much happening at one time. D said "mutha fucka I'm talking to you!" Snap I just regained consciousness. "First of all, you need to calm yo ass down. You know good and well I ain't no damn dog. And you better watch how you talking to me. I don't know what who ever that was is talking about. I ain't gotta cheat on you. If I needed to have sex with someone else I'd tell you that what we got going on ain't working and I'd leave." I hope she believed that cause if she don't I know it's over. She turned and walked away. I could hear her crying in the kitchen. I walked up behind her and put my arms around her. "Baby come on now you know me better than that. You know I love you. I'm here ain't I?" I did love her but I still had to lie bout the cheating. She turned around and hugged me back and said "I know baby, I'm sorry maybe it's just all that lying and cheating that I did messing with my mind making me think you out to do the same thing to me. I'll get over it. I love you too"

We went to sleep that night in each others arms. I felt good. But I kept thinking about who that was that called. I knew it wasn't Janai because I was dancing with her at the time so I figured it had to be Kay Kay. This bitch just don't get it. I should have killed her that night. But I was too busy worried about D. There were a lot of times that I could have killed her. As I slept that night I had about 10 dreams. Some of which I could remember very well.

Chapter 3:

Now in this dream (which was more like me remembering my past.) I was back in Atlanta (which is where I was from) with my ex and everything seemed to be cool. I was working and making a lot of money but I was also being a horrible girlfriend. I would leave for hours at a time and go hanging out in the bars getting with other girls. My ex didn't know at least that's what I thought until one night. I came home from one of my late nights and she had made dinner for me. She gave me a glass of wine. I kissed her forehead and began to eat. The steak she made me was good. As I ate I continued to sip my wine which was now making me drowsy and I was feeling a little light headed. But I figured it was just from the wine. The mashed potatoes looked so fluffy so I began to eat those too. While eating my steak it just seemed to melt in my mouth because my mouth was so watery. I looked down at it with my blurred vision and saw that as I cut into the meat it was leaking red juices. It was blood. I grabbed my napkin and started spitting out blood and wiping my tongue. But the more I wiped the more blood came out. My tongue was burning with every wipe. My head was spinning but when I looked at the mashed potatoes I could see little specks of light. I touched them and rubbed my fingers together and they started to bleed too. With my tongue hanging out my mouth bleeding I said in a muffled tone, "there's glass in this shit". She just sat there smiling at me. I wanted to jump up and slap the hell outta her but when I stood up and tried to reach across the table, I fell face first. I couldn't feel my legs. On the floor I propped myself up on my arms and tried to drag my body to the door. The bitch put something in my drink, gave me uncooked meat and put tiny pieces of broken glass in my damn potatoes. As I continued to slide my body closer to the door (as if she was gonna let me out) with blood still dripping form my mouth she grabbed my ankles and slid me back. "Where you going "baby" don't leave. We just getting started. The party is just getting crackin. Get it? Crackin, like what I'm bout to do to your ankles. I know, I know, you can't feel them right? But you will. Oh yeah, you will." She took the broom handle and began swinging and hittin me everywhere in my head, my legs (which I still couldn't feel yet) my arms and my back. And as she hit me she yelled one simple thing too me. "CHEATER" when she finished she left me laying there and went in the room and went to sleep. By the time I woke up it was the next day around 1 o'clock. There was a plate on the table with sausage and eggs and pancakes and a glass of orange juice for me. I wasn't touching none of it. My body was sore as hell My mouth was dry, tongue all swollen and it hurt like hell to stand. I just sat on the couch thinking about where she was at. Considering the fact that I couldn't walk all that well because of my ankles being swollen like baseballs, I sat there all day. When she walked through the door I tried to jump up but that was easier said than done. She sat down next to me and said "I think we should go our separate ways." YOU THINK!!!! we continued to talk and I said that everything was cool. *It wasn't.* I also told her that I understood her point of view, which I didn't. What I did understand and what I knew for a fact was that I wasn't fuckin with her no more. A few weeks later I moved to

California. Now even though it was in my dream this is what really happened to me and this is why I moved out here. I was just reliving it in my dream.

I remember tellin her that I fucked up and it was my bad but that if she ever needed anything to just call me. We couldn't ever be together again but after so many years of being in a relationship, you cant just let the friendship go like that. Maybe I deserved what she did to me that night. After I moved to California I got myself together but things started to slowly fall apart. I was trying to be good towards D and I really loved her but I slipped up a couple of times. Like when my ex called me one day and said she was getting put out of her apt. and had lost her job. She needed some where to stay. So like a fool I sent her a ticket to come out here. I told her she could stay with me for a while till she got a job and found a place. I also told her that I had a girlfriend. Seeing as how we were no longer together and just friends. I felt that I was in love again. (what the hell I tell her that for, I don't know.) She came out here and everything was cool the first couple of day's then she started getting mad because I was never there and I was always at my girl friends house. I had told D that my cousin came out here to live with me because she got into it with her mother. So along with the stripper lie, I lied about that too. Hell I couldn't tell my girlfriend that I moved my ex girl in with me. That's why I never took D to my house.

I remember after about a week of my ex being there she was sad and crying sitting on the balcony talking about how she missed home. I walked out there to try and comfort her and she gave me a hug while she was hugging me. She squeezed me tighter and tighter. Her hands started to move towards my ears and she started rubbing them. She knew that was my spot and I wouldn't be able to resist it. I tried to push her away but she pinned me against the wall. She unbuckled my belt and pulled my pants down.. she began massaging me and sliding her fingers in and out of me. That shit felt good. She was the only woman I ever let touch me like that and I kinda missed it. She got on her knees and put my left leg on her shoulder. Her tongue began to move on me and she began sucking and slurping in it like only she could. She was the only women I would ever let make me scream and call her name and I did just that. I began yelling Kay Kay. Once I reached my finishing point I pulled my pants up and walked away. Why did I let this happen. I couldn't believe myself. I knew I couldn't stay around her any more so I jumped in the shower and left. With D's mother dying that gave me a chance to get away and stay away. I had to be there for her anyway. Kay Kay got a job and met a new little girlfriend which was fine with me cause that meant she was one step closer to getting out my house. Now the crazy part was her new girlfriend was my girlfriend. I brought them around each other and everything. And didn't notice shit. How dumb was I. Them hoes was having a war and shit and I never connected the damn dots. I guess it was all my fuckin fault from the beginning. But they really don't know who they dealing with. I got this. D wanted to be a hoe so now I'm going to be one. They say two wrongs don't make a right but fuck that I'm making my own rules.

Chapter 4:

I jumped up early in the morning to my phone ringing. I looked around the room and D wasn't in there. Maybe it was her calling me. "Hello?" someone was crying on the other end "baby I'm sick. Come get me" the voice was drowned out by the crying so I couldn't tell who it was "D?" all of a sudden the crying stopped and the voice got clear. "No stupid it's me. I see she didn't leave yo sorry cheating ass yet. Don't worry she will." Click. She hung up the phone. Every time I wanna cuss her ass out she hang up the phone, damn. I swear if Kay Kay call me one more time I'ma find her and kill her. I could smell something cooking so I got up and walked in the kitchen. D was in there hooking it up. She just looked at me. "I got a call today." Here we go again. "Oh really from who baby" she wasn't smiling, "that bitch." I tried to play dumb but I knew who she was talking about. "What bitch?" "Yo skank ass cousin. She called my phone. She said she'd be back to finish the job." Damn think quick. "They still ain't caught her? Don't worry bout it she just talking" She slammed my plate down on the table as I sat down. She said "don't worry bout it? The crazy bitch shot me. *YOUR* cousin shot me and you want me to not worry bout it. I have to worry bout it since obviously your not. I gotta go. I'll be late coming home tonight. I gotta see my aunt bout some of my mom's things." And just like that she left. No kiss, no hug, or nothing, just a slam of the door. Seeing as how I just had a dream of what Kay Kay did to me with food, that plate stayed right there on that table, and I hopped in the shower. In the shower pictures ran flashed through my mind. Pictures of D smiling at me. Pictures of Kay Kay smiling at me and then in slow motion a picture of Janai went across my mind. Instantly I felt wet (and not from the water). I pictured her in the shower with me and me bending her over. Then the door bell rang. Damn it just broke my concentration. I got out and threw on a towel. Looking through the peep hole I could see Janai standing there. I thought my mind was trippin. So I squeezed my eyes shut and reopened them. She was still standing there. I opened the door and she said "well damn, I hope I *was* interrupting you. Taking a shower are we?" And with that she walked to the bathroom. With a giant smile on my face I locked the door and I followed slowly behind her and could see her taking her clothes off and jump in the shower. *At a time like this, whats a stud to do*? I grabbed my piece and put it on and walked into the bathroom. I pulled the shower door back and stepped in. she had her leg propped up and her fingers inside her. *Oh yeah, it's time to play*. I grabbed her hair and turned her around with my other hand and I bent her over. She didn't protest to any of it. I worked my way inside her and started to penetrate slow. My vision was coming true and it felt good. As I slowly worked my tool in and out of her I could hear her moaning. I let go of her hair and could see the water pounding on her back. As the water trickled down her body I could see her skin glistening. I continued to penetrate when I realized I was giving it to her the way I do D. She wasn't D and once again we wasn't in love. I grabbed her hair and pulled her head back towards my chest and started to hit it harder and harder. She started to scream, "fuck me Jay, fuck me." and she started bouncing it back at me. She was screaming so loud, I thought the neighbors could hear so I put my hands over her mouth. She tried to make a sound but it was muffled. I kissed her neck and whispered in her ear. "Shut the fuck up and take it." I moved my hand away and she said "OK daddy". I love it when they call me daddy. I beat it so long the water got cold and then I heard key's opening the door. **FUCK.**

Hearts beating a thousand miles per hour. I jumped so hard I hit my head on the shower door. Think. Shit. Think. What to do? It could only be D, cause the only person that had a key besides us was Janai and she was here. In the shower. With me. Damn. I placed my fingers to my lips telling Janai to be quiet and I jumped out the shower and tried to calmly walk into the living room. D was in there looking for something. "Hey babe what you doing back already?" She looked at me and said "I can't find my aunts key to her house it was in the pocket of my shirt I had on yesterday." OK all I gotta do is help her find her shirt. "Which shirt" She glanced up at me and said "the blue one with the silver necklace connected to it." She started to walk towards the room and I could feel my heart in my throat. Then she looked at me and said "go ahead and finish your shower I know you gotta get to work." I figured hey I'd be safer in the shower with Janai than letting D walk in and see her in there. So I gave her a kiss on the cheek and walked back in the bathroom. I looked and I could see Janai's silhouette in the shower. Damn she could have went out the window or something. As I started to take my towel off I saw D's shirt hanging on the back of the door. *YES*!
I grabbed it and took it too her and she smiled and said "thank you baby, hey I'm sorry bout earlier I'll make it up to you

tonight." She kissed me and left. That was close, I almost slipped up and got caught. I took my clothes off and jumped back in the shower. "She's gone so where were we?" Janai kissed my neck and said "you was scarred huh?" "Naw I just didn't want you getting your ass kicked. Before I got a chance to pound it out". At that point I finished handling my business with Janai and we both left the house and went our separate ways.

I got to work a little late but it was OK because my boss and I were cool. I was a little unfocused because of the morning I had and what a morning I had. It was crazy. Maybe I'm wrong for what I'm doing. Maybe D doesn't deserve to be going through this but hey she don't know shes going through it so maybe it's fine. I really don't wanna hurt her. But she hurt me too. 3 o'clock is taking too long to get here. It's only 12 but I think I'm going to leave early and go pick up D for lunch.

I get to D's job and wait in the parking lot for her to walk to her car. There she is, looking cute as hell in that red dress. I can see her smiling from here. She's so beautiful. I should be happy that I got her and I am but I don't know right now something feels funny about this whole situation. Right now is right now I'm going to take her to lunch and have fun.

As she hopped in the car she said " hey baby what brings you around here?" I grabbed her face and said "because I wanted to see you. I missed you all day." "You just saw me about three hours ago and you miss me already? Where we going?" I started the car and said "how bout some pancakes?" and smiled. "my favorite" she said as she gave me a kiss. Then her

phone rang it was a text message. And her smile soon faded. Then came the pain. Smack right across my face. I swerved through traffic and pulled to a stop in front of a store. "what the..." SMACK. Damn I couldn't even finish my sentence. "How many times?" I was speechless, what the hell is she talking about? "HOW MANY TIMES JAY?" she showed me a picture on her phone. It was a picture of me and Janai but you couldn't really tell it was Janai. "Who sent you that?" "Don't ask me no damn questions, I'm asking you the questions. Now how many times?" Do I lie? Or do I tell the truth? "uh twice". Tears fell out her eye's when she said "so I guess it all came back on me huh? I guess I was wrong about you huh? So what we had didn't mean shit to you either right?" She jumped out the car and started to walk down the street. I was stunned and all I could do was look at her walk away. I sat there thinking about how wrong I was from the gate and that I need to just come clean with her and let her know everything. But I was also thinking fuck that if she leave then she just leave and I'll just be alone and if she stay then that's fine too. I had a lot of thinking to do. While I thought about this situation if found myself fumbling through my phone and then it rang. "Hello?"
"Hey boo, did you miss me? Cause I missed you. When can I see you, daddy."It was Katrina. I figured what the hell maybe I can work it all out with her. "How bout now. Meet me at the burger stand by your old job, I'm sure you know where that is." She sounded surprised when she said "really, are you serious? OK, I'll be there in a min. I sat at the burger stand waiting for Kay Kay to show up. As I sat there my mind began to drift away. I began thinking about how this could play out. What had I gotten myself into. Trying to get back at D I dug myself

into a hole so deep it would take an army to get me out. As I continued to sit in the car with the music off tears began to fall from eyes. When I had to check myself. "Man up" I told myself. "Don't let no bitch get you down. This is the game your playing and damn't its your game. You play this shit the way you wanna play it." But the question was, did I really want to play it anymore? Was I getting tired? Could I handle being with someone and fucking their best friend and on top of that having my crazy ass ex stalking me. TAP TAP TAP. I jumped up and almost hit my head. It was Kay Kay. I pushed the button to unlock the door. She got in and looked at me and the first thing she said was "I'm sorry". Hell it's about time, I thought to myself. But instead I just looked at her and said "for". She sighed and said "for being a bitch and trying to ruin everything for you. But you hurt me. When I moved out here with you I thought we were going to work things out, then you told me you had a girl. And I wanted her to suffer the was I did. I knew you were a dog, I just needed to bring it out of you but I'm done now. I just have one more thing to do and I'm out ya life for good." I thought to myself "don't ask don't." "what's that?" I just had to ask. She began to smile when she said "meet me tomorrow night at the Red Rooster in Vegas. Here's your ticket through Southwest Airlines. If you meet me there and do everything I tell you to do, I promise I'm done and you can work on your relationship wit D" and with that she put the ticket on the seat and jumped out my truck and left. She didn't give me a chance to respond or nothing she just left. So she was playing her own game and I was being forced to play it with her.

Chapter 5

I drove home and tried to figure out what I was going to do. When I pulled up to the apt. I could see D's car so I pulled up behind it. As I walked in the house I could smell something and it made me hungry as hell. D was standing by the stove stirring a something in a big pot. She had on some high heeled shoes a purple thong and the laced bra to match. So now she made me hungry and horny. Oh Boi. I walked over to her and gave her a kiss on the cheek. She just turned her head. She was playing hard to get, OK we can play. So I went into the room and took my clothes off then I hopped in the shower. I had to had been in there for 30 min or more. When I got out I could hear my favorite love making CD playing which made me excited. I stepped into the room and didn't see D. I figured she was still cooking cause the aroma had gotten stronger. But after I put on my sports bra and boxers and walked into the living room I noticed she was gone. I walked over to the kitchen and looked in the pot and I'll be damned if there was nothing in the pot. Just water and seasonings. The mutha fucka cooked water with seasoning salt and pepper and left. She got me hungry as hell and played me, I went to sleep. When I woke up the next morning D was still gone so I decided I would take the trip to Vegas. I needed to get Kay Kay out my life for good.

Steppin out the airport in Las Vegas, Nevada it was hot as hell. I began to sweat instantly. It was so hot I felt like I was in a sauna and someone turned the heat up. As I walked to the closest cab I saw my phone rang. It was D. "Hello?" "Hey Jay listen when you get home tonight I need to talk to you OK?" I was just shocked that she called me. "OK no problem, I mean that's cool, I love you see you tonight." She paused for a second and "I love you too see you later." I looked at the cab driver and said "Do you know where the Hot Rooster is?" He looked back at me and started smiling. Then he shook his head and started to drive. Now when I pulled up I thought it was a regular bar or club because the windows were tinted black. The lady at the booth said "$10 please." I handed her the money and the door opened automatically the lady said "have a nice time". As I walked in I could see neon signs everywhere even though it was dark in there. I could also see a stripper pole in the middle of the floor but I began to become even more shocked as I walked around. Every where I turned people were kissing and rubbing on each other. As I walked down a long hallway there were doors with large windows on them on each side. As I glanced into one of the rooms it looked like a doctors office. I could see a girl laying on the exam table and a man standing over her with a doctors coat on and his dick in her mouth. What the hell? I kept walking and the next room I looked into looked like a class room. I could see 3 naked female students and three female teachers standing over them with straps on that were shooting out white stuff. WOW. I kept walking and the next room looked like a cave. There was a girl chained to the wall and another girl in a handstand position chained against her. The guy was standing there with a whip and making sure they continued the 69 until he was done masturbating. This shit is crazy. I kept walking to the end of the hallway where I saw a jacuzzi filled with people licking and sucking on each other. One guy was sitting back in the tub while a girl bounced on his lap and another girl was behind her stroking the first girls ass with a strap. And in the mist of everything Kay Kay was sitting in the jacuzzi naked watching everything. She turned and looked at me and said. "Take your clothes off and get in." This was crazy but I knew I had to, so I did. So off came the clothes. And I slid my body into the water. Damn the water felt good. I closed my eyes tight and opened them when I felt someone sit on my lap. Damn it was Janai. What the hell is she doing here? This was all bad but it felt all good. Janai stood up and Kay Kay handed me a strap. I looked at her and she pushed the strap into my chest. I guess that meant put it on. So I did. Kay Kay pointed at Janai and said "ride it" Janai looked like she didn't want to but she did. She sat back on my lap slowly and began to wind her way down. It started to feel good. I guess she started feeling good also because I could hear her moaning and that made my body loose control. I put my hands on her waist and began to help her as I started pumping harder from under her. She started getting louder and louder.

We continued on doing the things that she asked us to do. As the night went on I began to wonder why she just wanted me and Janai to have sex and why she didn't want to be involved I started to get tired and ready to go home when Kay Kay looked at me and said your free to leave when your ready. "I said well hell I'm ready now." as Janai got up to grab her clothes she said "me too." "Well leave then" Kay Kay said as she turned and walked away. Janai and I looked at each other, then back at her and said we will soon as you give us our tickets. Kay Kay flipped her hair back, turned back towards us and said "I just got you here. You can get yourselves back." She laughed as she walked away. Janai looked at her and said bitch I only played your game because I wanted to but you being disrespectful is gonna get ya ass kicked. Kay Kay said "fuck you" and continued to walk out the door. Janai looked at me and then she kissed me and said I'll be back. She ran out the door and by the time I could get out there behind her she was already slamming Kay Kay's head into a trucks doors. Damn why they gotta be fighting and shit in a whole other state. Part of me wanted Janai to beat that ass so I watched for a second. After about a minute I grabbed her arm and pulled her to the side and said we gotta go. We ran to the street and flagged down a taxi. "Airport please" I told the cab driver. And we were gone. At the airport we saw that all flights going back to L.A. Were booked until the next morning so we rented a car. We were only about 4 hours from home driving so that was fine. On the way home we talked. We actually talked a lot. I found out a lot about D and how they met. And how they came out together and also how they were each others firsts. I bet that was some sexy shit. I would have loved to watch that. So I just had to ask her why me. Why was she fuckin me when I was with her best friend. She began to explain it to me. " Well I think you are fine as hell and that night we all met, you pushed me to the left to get at her and she ain't even all that fine. Then to top it all off she stopped our little every now and then flings to be with you and then cheated on you. She's selfish and only cares about her self. Not you, me or anybody else. So she needs to learn a lesson and I figured I could teach her one." Wait, "did you just say before she got with me y'all was still getting busy?" I asked her. "Yeah, see the deal was if I ain't got nobody and she don't got nobody then we got each other." Damn. If that ain't a deal right there. This shit was crazy. So Janai was only fuckin me to get back at D. I think I feel used. But feeling used kinda feels good. I dropped Janai off at her car at the airport and hopped in mine and we went our separate way's and I headed home. I wondered what would happen when I got there. I didn't have to wonder too long though cause soon I was pulling up to the apt. and her car wasn't there. So I guessed nothing would happen. As I walked in the house I felt a since of calm come over me. Tonight was gonna be a good night. I guess I was wrong about that because as I walked in the room D was laying on the bed with her hands tied to the head board and her legs wide open and all I could see was blood. Blood came from her face around her mouth. Her eyes were black and swollen. Her clothes were ripped and she was bleeding between her legs. Starring at her and screaming her name I began to dial 911 on my cell phone. As I tried to pat her cheeks I could hear the sirens. When the paramedics rushed in the room their heads dropped and I thought she was dead. One of them touched her neck and said "WE GOT A PULSE" they cut the rope that had her tied up and put her on the gurney and into the ambulance. With light's and sirens whaling we raced to the hospital. The same hospital that held her mother only a year ago when she died. My heart was racing and all I could think about as what a fucked up situation we were both in and how I wanted to make it right with her.

Chapter 6:

At the hospital the police came and had a million and one questions. And slowly but surely the questions began to sound like I was a suspect. FUCK. The officer pulled me to the side and asked me all kind of questions like "when you called you said you came home and she was already like this right"? "Yes" I said. I wondered if he could hear the fear in my voice. He looked at me and said "so where were you coming from and who was with you that can testify that you were with them"? Damn this can't be good because either way it goes this could end up all bad. But damn that, I ain't going to jail for nobody. "I was in Vegas with a friend." The cop looked me up and down, wrote something on his notepad then said "and this friends name would be and how can I get in contact with them"? Shit think, and think quick. Do I tell the truth? "Janai, but I don't know her last name" the officer gave me a look as if to say AND so then I said "and Katrina" and I gave him their numbers. The officer said "thank you for your cooperation and we will be in contact with you all again soon." He tried to shake my hand but I walked away and back into the room with D. When she wake's up from this it's gonna be a done deal. And I'm thinking I know who did it to her but I just don't know how. Kay Kay was with us in Vegas, even though she did get on the plane to home and we had to drive so she should have been back about an hour before us. This shit is insane. When ever D gets better and good enough to come home everything is gonna go bad.

It's been three weeks and D is still in the hospital but the doctor said she can go home today and I'm happy bout that but at the same time I'm a little worried. As I walked in her hospital room I could see Janai and GiGi helping her get her things together. I pulled a wheel chair close to the bed and helped her get in it when a lady walked in the room. "Hi, I'm detective Shaw" she said as she extended her hand to D. D shook her hand while saying "hello" as they released the hand shake detective Shaw went right into the reason for her visit. "I just wanted to let you know we caught the person who did this to you and we need you to come identify her." "Her"? I asked "Yes, do you know a Katrina White"? D shook her head and said "yeah, I know her ass". "OK well good she's being held with no bail and were going to court in a week. If you can remember anything about that night it would be great. A lawyer will be getting in contact with you soon". With that she turned and walked away. We got D's discharge paperwork and left the hospital.

On the way home I asked D if she was hungry. "Naw I just wanna go home." So we drove home in silence. And I contemplated if I should tell her everything. But I figured now was not the best of times. She was just getting home from being in the hospital. But hell, when would be the appropriate time to say "I'm fucking your best friend and by the way the girl who is supposed to be my cousin and tried to kill you twice is actually my crazy ass ex girlfriend. But I love you and want us to work it out." I'm in such a fucked up position. And the worst part is I did it to myself. We got to the house and I helped D out the car. As I opened the house door she kind of pulled her arm away from me. I started to wonder why and when I got ready to open my mouth to ask her what the problem was she threw her hand up behind her as to say shut the fuck up and don't talk to me. I felt like she just checked me with out saying anything. What kind of shit is that. Did she just shh me? I think she did. Now my head is all fucked up. I don't know what to think but I'm hoping that its just cause she's tired and she's just getting home. So I'm just gonna try and make the best of it and keep her happy. When she walked in the room and noticed the roses on the pillow that I left for her I could see her smile.

For the next few day's I waited on her hand and foot I even bought her a bell that she could ring for me when she needed me. She began to even get up and slowly walk around. I took time off from work so I didn't have to leave her alone at all. And within just those few day's we started to get back to that fresh new couple that we used to be. Learning each other again and falling in love again. And it was actually new to us because we both had never given each other our all. I was giving her 110 percent and she was giving me the same. It felt great.

When it came time for court we were back to where we should have been the whole time. Sitting next to her in the court room I was a little nervous. Especially when I saw Kay Kay walk in the room in her jump suit with her hands shackled. She looked at us and had a seat next to her lawyer. And the bailiff asked us to please rise for the judge to come into the courtroom. They called D to the stand. She squeezed my hand and stood up and slowly walked up there. They swore her in and she sat down. Immediately they began to drill her with questions like how did she know Katrina and what happened that night as she answered all of the questions I could see her eyes began to fill with tears and you could hear the cry in her voice but she pushed it back and continued to answer the questions. By the time they finished with her I was tired and wanted to cry. Once she sat down they brought up the paramedics from that night and questioned them about her condition when they arrived. After that the judge ordered a recess. And we went into the courts cafeteria. While we were in their Janai walked up to us. We were both shocked. "What are you doing here"? D asked. Janai looked at me apologetically and said I was summoned to come in today, I guess cause I'm your best friend. And no matter what I'm your best friend right"? She looked at D asking. D said yeah girl you my nigga fo life, shit thanks for coming hopefully this bitch gets locked up fo a lifetime, you feel me" It was now time for us to go back in the courtroom. Hell hopefully Janai gets up there and lies her ass off bout everything. Cause I cannot afford for things to mess up now. We all sat down and had to stand back up for the judge to come back in. Once she sat down we were instructed to sit down and Janai was called to the stand. Here we go. The Lawyer asked her the first question. "How do you know the defendant."? Janai said she was messing with my best friend. "So when you say messing with you mean sexually or in a harming way"? Janai looked at D and said "sexually". Then the lawyer asked "and do you know where the defendant Katrina White was on the night in question"? Janai hung her head down and said a quiet "yes". "Speak up please we can't hear you" "YES". "Thank you and can you please tell the court where she was that night" with her head still down she said "In Vegas with me". D's head popped back and she looked at me and I was speechless. As Janai began to explain the Vegas situation D began to release my hand and she slowly got up and ran out the court room all I could do was look at Janai and ask why with my eyes. And she just held her head down. The judge let every one leave for the day and told us to be back tomorrow morning. Kay Kay walked out the courtroom with the biggest smile on her face. I guess she happy and her plan worked. I raced out after D. but she was gone and so was my car. I was stuck. Janai offered me a ride but I couldn't talk to her, all I could do was just walk away with my head down and my hand in my pockets. I walked to the bus stop and when the bus pulled up I hopped on and headed home. When I got there the door was wide open I peaked my head in and I saw a pot flying my way. I hurried up and pulled my head back. Do I really want to walk in here? Well fuck it here I go.

I walked in with my hands in the air and begin pleading "baby baby let me explain". A cup passes my ear. Without looking at me D says "explain, explain, yeah tell me what the fuck you need to explain" as another pot passes my head. I'm in a fuckin war zone. She has really gone crazy cause she tearing up her own shit. Once again I put my hands up and said "baby calm down. I'm bout to explain". And just then Janai walks through the door and say's "no let US explain". Oh my God this bitch is not helpin. D looks up and says "oh bitch you got me fucked up, you know what come on in here". She starts walking towards her closet. And I know what she keeps in her closet.

Janai said "oh shit so you gonna go to the closet on me? You just said I was your nigga fo life". D stops in her track and falls to the floor and starts crying. "What the fuck am I doing? I'm going crazy. I feel like I'm loosing my mind". She starts slapping her head and we begin to walk closer to her. In my opinion as long as she ain't went in the closet we should both be straight. Without looking up D say's "How long"? We both seemed puzzled by the question, so I said "how long what? D gave me the coldest look when she said "how long have you been screwing my *EX* best-friend"? We started to stutter with the answer when D said "y'all wasn't stuttering when y'all was fucking so how long"? I guess it took too long for an answer this time cause D raised her leg and kicked Janai so hard in her stomach that she flew almost to the kitchen. D jumped up and ran over to Janai and grabbed her by her hair with one hand while she repeatedly hit her face with her free fist. I ran over to them and tried to stop the fight which by now was a rumble cause Janai was hittin back, when D turned around and hit me in my eye. At this point I was going to just walk away but then she pushed me into the wall and started to hit me in my face. There was no walking away now so I grabbed her by her neck and slammed her into the wall. "Calm the fuck down". As I released the grip on her neck I slowly sat down and said we need to talk about this shit calmly damn, chill out for a second". D sat down where she was at. And out of no where Janai jumps in D's face an bangs her head into the wall yelling "BITCH, don't you ever forget who I am. I'm dat pop off bitch. I kick asses for you not the other way around. Shit I was just tryna see if what you was getting from her was as good as you said it was. I just wanted you to fuckin hurt the way you had me hurtin when you decided you wanted to be in committed relationship and then you turned around and cheated on her and it wasn't even with me. You cheated with some random ass female. What kind of shit is that. So fuck yo feelings right now cause mine is hurt to. When you get those thoughts together and you ready to talk to me bout it like a women then we can talk, until then I'm gone." She turned around and walked out the door. D started to jump up after her and I grabbed her arm and told her to let it go and sit down and talk to me about this situation. D looked at me and said quietly "I'm going to get up now and I'm going to my closet. When I am done getting what I need to get you better not be in my sight. She started to stand up and I grabbed her arm but she just pulled it away and went towards the closet. A women scorned. I'm outta here. I got up and walked out the door. I really didn't have no where to go that night so I just got me a room at a local motel. I laid in the bed thinking, what a day. And to top it off I gotta go to court tomorrow and get on the stand and talk about how I actually know Kay Kay.

Just as I changed the channel of the T.V. there was a knock at the door. Must be the management or something cause no one knows that I'm here. Once I got to the door and looked out the peep hole I could see D standing there in a long ass trench coat that went to her ankles. As I opened the door, I said "Babe, what are you doing here? Are you OK? She put her finger to my lips and said "shh" she dropped her coat and jumped into my arms. Oh my God she's naked. She starts kissing me as I walk backwards into the room kicking the door closed. I didn't know why she was doing what she was doing and I didn't care.

All I knew was my baby was here. Naked. And I was carrying her, and kissing her and at this point I was still standing and lifting her up, placing her legs on my shoulders and taking her into my mouth. As her body made circles on my face I could feel her warm juices flow onto my tongue. The room starts to spin and colors begin to flash. Just the thought of knowing that I'm giving her pleasure took me to ecstasy and beyond and I knew that at that point I was truly in love with her and sorry for everything that I put her through. I laid her on the bed and began caressing her body all over when the door opened and it was Janai standing there in the same trench coat I tried to jump up but D pulled me closer to her kissing me all over my neck. Janai walked in and closed the door. She took her place on the bed and started licking and sucking on D's breast. I was shocked. I was having a three some with my girl and her best friend. And I was handling it. Once again the door slammed open this time it was Katrina but she wasn't there to join in. She was holding a gun in each hand. As the shots blasted all over the room I felt a sharp piercing pain in my chest. I was hit. How did she get out of jail. How did this happen. Janai and D were screaming. Blood was leaking all over the place I could feel myself drifting in and out of consciousness and just then at that very moment, I woke up grabbing my chest with sweat dripping down my face. That wasn't just a dream that was a nightmare. Damn my shirt soakin wet, my heart beating all fast. I ain't going back to sleep no time soon, but I am tired as hell. Imma just lay here. If I fall asleep then fine but I ain't rushing nothing.

Chapter 7:

Beep Beep Beep. Oh my God if my alarm don't stop going off. I hate when I set my alarm on my phone cause it don't stop till it feels like it half the time. I guess I gotta get up now. My head is killing me though. Court is going to be long and hard. I guess it's now or never. Here I go. I took a long shower and tried to clear my mind but it didn't work. Too many thoughts were flowing through it. As I got dressed I thought about how much I really did care about D and how I fucked up. I mean I messed up from the beginning. It was just one big lie followed by what seemed like a million small lies. I threw my clothes on and locked the door. As I walked past the office I slid the room key through the slot in the window. I jumped in my car and drove towards the freeway. Rolling on the freeway I listened to all D's favorite songs and wondered if she was going to show up for court today. Something inside of me was kind of glad all of this was out in the open now and that I didn't have to hide anything anymore. Yet something ached inside of me. I felt horrible for all the pain I had put her through. Even though she cheated on me, I feel it was my fault. If I would have never let Katrina crazy ass come live with me then none of this would have happened. Pulling up to the court building I could feel my heart jump. I could feel it pounding in my chest and shortly after that it was in my throat. It's hot as hell outside. I feel like I'm sweating my ass off and I just got out the car. Walking into the courtroom was cold. And not just the temperature. The people were the coldest part. The way they looked at me as I walked in and found a seat. Looking around the courtroom I could see D who wouldn't look at me. GiGi was sitting next to her, he did look at me. If his eyes were a knife I would a horizontal slice right at my neck the way he just cut them at me. As I continued to scan the room, I didn't see Janai or Kay Kay. Which was a good thing I guess. The judge entered the room and the bailiff said a loud "All RISE". Here we go. The attorney said "I'd like to call Jaydin Pierce to the stand. I stood up and slowly walked up to the stand. I put my hand on the bible and even that was cold. As they swore me in that lump in my throat got bigger. I sat down and the questions began. "Ms. Pierce, do you know Donna Jones?" "Yes" "And how do you know Ms. Jones". "She's my girlfriend", "EX". GiGi yelled out. "QUIET IN THE COURT" the judge said as she slammed down her gavel. The Attorney then asked me about Katrina and how I knew her. "Well I met her about 5 years ago in Atlanta, GA. She is my ex girlfriend". I could see D's face drop and I could see her lay her head on GiGi's shoulder.

---

1 year later

Dear D,

I know you probably don't want to hear or read this but I'm writing it anyway and hopefully one day you'll read it and understand with an open heart and mind what I am trying to say to you.

    Now in the beginning I fucked up. I lied to you from the gate. I told you that Katrina was my cousin. I should have just been honest with you. For that I deeply apologize. I know that I hurt you in more ways than I can think of and I'm sorry for that also. The whole thing with Janai didn't mean anything to me. I just did it because it was something to do and I called myself trying to hurt you for cheating on me, not realizing that I was at fault too. In spite of everything when I told you that I loved you I meant it. I know it doesn't mean much now but I did. It took everything going wrong for me to understand that.

    I'm not asking for you to give me a second chance or anything like that. I'm not even asking for you to respond to this letter. I'm just asking you to believe the words that I am saying to you. I don't know if you are in a relationship right now or not and if you are I mean no disrespect. I just wanted you to know how I felt.

Take care Donna Jones.

Sincerely,

Jay :)

It's been a year since I last seen D and I wrote this letter for her just so she knows how I feel. The last time I saw her we were in court and I just broke the news to her bout Katrina. She didn't even stay to hear the judges decision. She got up and walked out the court. That was the last I saw or heard from her. Katrina ended up getting some major time for what she did to D both times. Thank God. I haven't seen Janai either. Neither one of them have been by the club. I've talked to a few girls but I just couldn't get serious with anyone. So I haven't been lonely just been alone. I'll put this letter in the mail on my way to work. Hell I don't even know if she still lives in the same place. So if it gets to her that's good, if not hey it was worth the shot. I wonder if she got a girl if she do I hope she happy. Enough reminiscing, time to get ready for work. I'll grab something to eat on the way there. I put the letter in the outgoing mail on my mail box and jumped in my car to head to the preschool.

With my music bumping loud I started on my 15 min journey to work. I seemed to be making every light too so I figured it was gonna be a good day. I pulled into my favorite burger stand and ordered me a breakfast burrito and a large orange soda boppin my head the whole time, paid the lady and I was out. Listening to 2pac keep ya head up noddin my head and eating my burrito I passed through the intersection with not a care in the world when this car black car with a pink front license plate came speeding running a red light. It hit my truck so hard it did a 360 turn in the middle of the intersection. Unconscious the paramedics rushed me to the hospital which is where I've been the last 3 day's. What I didn't now and would have never guessed was that D has been here the last 2 days sitting with me. See when I filed out my insurance paper work a year and a half ago I put D as my emergency contact. And seeing as how this was an emergency they called her. I just didn't understand why she came.

Day 4 I open my eyes for the first time since I entered the hospital to see D sleeping with her head rested at the foot of the bed. I tried to kick my foot but it barely moved. It moved enough for D to shoot her head up, look my way and yell "NURSE". The nurses ran in and began doing things to me and D faded out of the room. I still couldn't talk so I couldn't call her name. Was I dreaming? Was she really there. Once the nurses left out and all the tubes were out of my body I tried to sit up in the bed but it wasn't working. D walked in the room. She saw me struggling and pushed the button to raise my back. I just looked at. "What are you doing here"? I asked her. "I don't know". She said as she got up and went into the restroom. She walked back into the room wiping her eyes with tissue. "They called me so I came to make sure you were OK. But now that your woke I see I cant do this. I gotta go. I'll be back tomorrow to check on you. She turned around grabbed her purse and walked out the door. The rest of the day was filled with silence for me. Just me and my thoughts. No one to talk to or listen to me talk. The next morning came quick and I got a couple of calls from a couple of people I knew from work and then around 12 D came by the hospital. When she walked through the door she had a card in her hand. "Ahh that is so sweet you shouldn't have". I told her. She looked at me and said "oh but I didn't this is for your nurse". The smile on my face dropped. Then she quickly said "I'm just messing with you, here you go." Then she kissed me on my cheek and handed me the card. I opened it and read it as she sat down. It felt good to see her here and have her kiss me again. Maybe we can work things out. Hopefully we can eventually but for right now this is good. She found something on the small T.V. and we sat there and watched it not really saying too much to each other but every time I tried to adjust myself she jumped to help me out. She stayed with me all day made sure I was warm an everything. Towards the evening before she got ready to go she said "I got your letter in the mail today, thank you and no, I don't have a girl right now I'm just tryna do me right now. I don't need to be in a relationship. I'm cool by myself. Hell maybe one day but after all a relationship has put me through I'm fine by myself. But I'm glad to see that you have changed some what. How bout we work on being friends for right now and you work on getting out of this hospital aight. See you tomorrow". She got up kissed my cheek again and walked out the room. Damn I see my mistakes why can't she see just give another chance. All I wanna do is make it right with her and show her that I could really love her right. All those thoughts flowing through my mind made me tired, mostly cause I didn't sleep throughout the day. I didn't want to miss a moment with D. For as long as she wants to be around I want her around and I want her to stay in my life. I wanna make it right. I'm guessing now is as good a time as any.

Chapter 8:

Lessons Learned Pt. 2...

Today is a great day. Dr. Brown said I can go home, so I am happy as hell. My walking is still a little slow but hell I'mma be outta here so I ain't trippin. I called the cab about 20 minutes ago so it should be here soon. After the nurse brought in my discharge papers I gathered my things together and in walked D. looking as beautiful as ever. Wearing a big ass smile. "Hey Jay, so I hear they letting you out finally. Good shit." "Yeah I'm ready to. My cab is on it's way so you almost missed me." Her smile turned upside down when she said "Cab, why would you call a cab instead of me? Well whatever I'm here now so ain't no need for a damn taxi. Get ya stuff so I can take you home." When she saw the way I was still limping she ran over to me and put her arm around my waist and my arm over her shoulder and we walked out the hospital. As she helped me into the car she asked "where do you live"? I gave her the directions and she drove me there. I had completely forgot that we hadn't seen each other in a year since she was with me the whole time I was in the hospital. So she hadn't seen my new spot or anything. When we pulled up she asked me for my keys and said she was going to open the door and for me to wait for her till she got back so she could help me out. I gave her my keys and waited for her to come back to the car but she was taking along time. At first I thought it was because you kind of had to jiggle the key a little bit to open the door but when I noticed that it was taking too long I decided to get out and go see what was wrong. And just as I got out the car she came with a bag and said "didn't I say stay in the car? That's your problem you don't listen. Now get back in the car." "What's in the bag"? She smiled and said "your clothes, you coming with me. Your gonna stay at my house till you can walk better and everything cause you look pitiful and I can't just leave you like that." I sat back in the car and we drove to her house. I laid my head back against the head rest and said so where you living now? You still in the same spot"? She shook her head and said "Nope, I had to upgrade from that spot too many bad memories, you feel me. To be honest with you I don't even live out here anymore." "What where you live now"? "Not even taking her eyes off the road she said "Rancho." I didn't even know where that was. I had heard of it but had never been. "How far is that"? "About 45 min" damn she drove that far everyday just to come see me in the hospital. I think I got a chance with her. I laid my head back and just watched the mountains pass by. I don't know what I'm getting into but I hope it ends up with me and her making it work for real this time.

Once off the freeway we made a few turns and I saw a bunch of houses lined up that looked just alike. They were all peach colored and and every other one was a two story house. We pulled into the third single story house that had little lights that stuck out of the ground and lined the stone pathway to the front door. She pulled into the driveway and pushed the button for her garage door to open. As I got out the car I was once again impressed. I was also kind of sad that she didn't get this with me. We should have got this together. Unfortunately I was the one who fucked everything up. I walked into her house and was amazed with the way it was decorated. D always did have a certain sense of style that could make any place look worth a million bucks. She gave me the grand tour of the house. First we went into the kitchen that was designed with all black and stainless steel appliances. We then went into the den area that wasn't decorated all that much. It only had a couch in it. "I haven't had a chance to do anything in here, mostly because I got that T.V. in there that I want to put on the wall and don't know how and then I got a coffee table and some end tables that came in a damn box and I don't know how to do that shit either. But it will get up there eventually. Come on let me take you to the rest of the house". It was a three bedroom house so she showed me her guest room where I would be sleeping at which was nice. The other room she said she was going to make her office. It was pretty much empty too. Then she showed me to her master bed room. And man it was big. Her bedroom and bathroom was red and black with silver thrown in here and there. We went back into the room that was going to be mine and she helped me get situated. She brought my things in and said she would put them away while I took my shower. I got in the shower and stayed in there for about 20 min just thinking about the day, and where I was at. It felt good in the water and even better to be out that hospital. I never thought I would need someone to take care of me, and I especially never thought that the person would be the very one that I put through so much hell. I got out and D wasn't in the room so I put on the underwear that was on the bed, and got in the bed. As I laid there I began to flip through the channels of the T.V. and found something that caught my eye. I could feel myself starting to dose off when I heard the room door open. D walked in with a glass of water and a pill bottle. She told me to sit up so I could take the medicine. As I sat up she handed me the cup and medicine and climbed in the bed next to me. We laid there in the bed all night watching T.V. till I eventually fell asleep. When I woke up in the morning D was still sleep so I got out the bed slowly and walked into the living room. She had boxes of stuff stacked neatly in the corner. Why had she not unpacked yet? I know she can't be that busy that she don't have time to unpack. I just looked through a couple and I could see pictures of her mom and her when she was little and some of her awards from school. At her old apt she didn't have any of these up so I figured it was because her apt was too small or something. I kept looking at the pictures for a while when I heard her walk in behind me. "So you going through my things huh"? I turned around and said "my bad I saw a picture hanging out of a box and looked at it. Then I noticed that there were more and I just wanted to see what you looked like when you were little. I didn't even know you had these pictures". As she picked up one and looked at it she said "yeah, I just got all these boxes from my aunts house it used to be my moms. So I decided that I would put it up in this house. You know, kinda keep her me close to her." She turned around to leave and said " I need to get ready for work but feel free to look around and make yourself comfortable. Eat what ever you want but I'll bring something home for dinner." As she walked into the kitchen I watched her body sway from left to right. And it made me want her, though I knew I couldn't have her. At least not right now any way. I could hear her in the shower singing loud to the music that was playing in the bathroom. I just laughed to myself and went back into the room. My back hurt so I decided to lay down for a while and ended up dozing off.

I woke up to the sounds of the T.V. The house was empty. I was all alone. D didn't even wake me up when she left. There was a note on the nightstand though, and it said *"See you later sweetie, make sure you rest good. I'll be back around 6. "D"."*
She called me sweetie. Yeah Boi. I got up and went into the kitchen and found something to eat. As I sat at the table and I thought about all the things that happened, I tried harder to think about how to make all of them right. I walked into the Den and opened the closet door. I could see the boxes for the coffee table and end table and decided I should put them together. So I searched the house for some tools. When I found them I went to work. Seeing as how my body still wasn't at a hundred percent it took a hell of a lot longer than expected. I'm talking so long that I didn't finish till damn near 4. Well I took some breaks in between. When I finally finished I contemplated putting the T.V. on the wall. That shit looked hard. But hell why not try so it did. And you know what I got it up there. By the time I finished everything it was almost 6. I went in the room and sat on the bed I didn't want to fall asleep though because I wanted to be up when she got home. That didn't work. I think as soon as I sat down I fell asleep. I woke up to D kissing me on my cheek. For someone who don't want a relationship she sure is affectionate and physical. But hey I like that. "Hey you. You been sleep all this time"? She said smiling. Wiping my eyes like I just been sleep for 14 hours I said "naw I was up for a while, actually I just went to sleep"
She stood up and said well come on in the kitchen I brought dinner. As we walked into the kitchen and passed the den she glanced in and saw everything set up she turned around and damn near jumped in my arms. "OUCH ouch ouch" She

almost broke my back. "Oh shit I'm sorry". Then she hit my shoulder talking bout "how you do all this and you were supposed to be resting. How long did it take"? "All day but it was worth it." We sat at the table and ate and talked and it felt like old times. When we finished we went into the room and she got my things while I took a shower. It didn't take me long. D was laying in the bed. I thought she would sleep in her bed tonight but OK. I climbed in the bed and laid my head on the pillow. She placed her leg across me and turned on her stomach. Laid there for a second and then climbed on top of me. She placed the sweetest kiss on my lips and then my neck. Her tongue began to make circles all over my body and she worked her way down. Did I want this to happen? I normally don't let this happen but it felt great. She went where only few have been and at that moment I knew I was going to make her mine again. No more screwing up for me I got to wife this one. She came up to my ear and whispered "don't ever hurt me again. I got to you once I can get to you again. Black car. Pink License Plate". She continued licking all over me. DAMN. As I turned her over I looked in her eye's and said "I guess that's a *Lesson Learned...*"

Yeah she got me. She got me bad. Hospitalized me in all, but you know what I think I liked it. It's something bout the crazy ones...

Lessons Learned Pt. 2...

Thanks to all of you for your purchase. This is my second book in my Lesson's Learned... Series. I hope you all enjoyed it and I hope it was as much fun reading this as it was for me writing it. More to come...

-King Shortie

www.ingramcontent.com/pod-product-compliance
Lightning Source LLC
Chambersburg PA
CBHW061226280526
45784CB00006B/2655